The Simple 3-Step Secret to Slaughter Writer's Block

And Vanquish it Forever

By

Christopher di Armani

http://ChristopherDiArmani.net/Books
author@ChristopherDiArmani.net

ISBN-13: 978-0-9879345-3-6
ISBN-10: 0987934538

Published By:

Botanie Valley Productions Inc.
PO Box 507
Lytton, BC V0K 1Z0
http://BotanieValleyProductions.com

Dedication

First and foremost this book is dedicated
to my sweet and loving wife Lynda.
Without her unwavering support
none of this would be possible.

Second, this book is dedicated to every writer who
finds themselves at a loss for words.

It's okay.

There is a cure and it's far simpler than you ever imagined.

You'll see.

Table of Contents

Foreward...9

Defining The Problem 13

Writer's Block Takes Many Forms 17

    Blank Page Syndrome 17

    I Can't Come Up With an Idea! 18

    I Have Too Many Ideas...19

    My outline isn't finished or my outline isn't perfect yet. 19

    I Don't Know What Happens Next...20

    People Will Say This Story Sucks..21

    My Characters are Dull and Boring 21

    My Inner Editor Says I Suck 22

    Fear of Failure..23

    Fear of Rejection 23

    Fear of Success...25

    What do these forms of Writer's Block have in common? 26

Popular Yet Ineffective Coping Mechanisms..29

    Talking With Other Writers 29

    Class Discussion 29

    Group Discussion...30

    Journaling...30

    List Making..31

    Brainstorming...31

    Mind-Mapping 31

    Free Association Writing 31

    Stop Writing...32

    Get out of Your Chair, Dance, Run or Walk....................................32

Eliminate Distractions 33

Write Early in the Morning 33

Write Late at Night 33

Write at a Different Time Each Day 34

Write While You Sleep 34

The Glass of Water Technique 34

Waiting for Inspiration 35

I'm Too Tired 35

Talk to Your Imaginary Friend 35

Swear like a Trucker 35

Use a Different Writing Tool 36

Take A Trip 36

The Caffeine Slam 37

Write Somewhere Else 37

Write in Your Local Bookstore 38

Wash the Dog 38

Wash the Car 38

Shut Off Your Computer 39

Browse Old Photo Albums 39

Play on Facebook 39

Re-Read Your Best Work 40

Start in the Middle of the Story 40

Take a Smoke Break 41

Listen to the Rain Pelt Down on a Tin Roof 41

Steal Someone Else's Idea 41

Read a Book 42

Listen to Music 42

Read Inspirational Quotes 42

Defining The Solution To Writer's Block 43

Slaying The Demon of Writer's Block 45

    Step 1 - Plant Your Buttocks in Your Writing Chair 47

    Step 2 - Set a Deadline 49

    Step 3 - Write 51

    That's It. 54

Actions Guaranteed to Help 55

    Face The Truth About Writing 55

    Write Every Day 56

    Write From an Outline 58

    Schedule a Specific Time to Write 59

    Create Mini-Deadlines For Yourself 62

    Minimize Distractions 63

    Listen to Non-Verbal Music 64

    Create Your Personal Writing Sanctuary 65

Final Thoughts 67

One Last Thing! 69

About Christopher di Armani 70

Books by Christopher di Armani 73

"There is no such thing as writer's block
for writers whose standards are low enough."

— William Stafford

Foreward

"There's no such thing as writer's block. That was invented by people in California who couldn't write."

— Terry Pratchett

Writer's Block is a catch-all term applied to a whole host of maladies, real and imagined. They cripple amateur and professional writers alike.

Why?

Clarity of purpose.

More specifically, a *lack* of clarity of purpose.

Midnight Disease, Blank Page Syndrome, Writer's Burnout and Paralysis by Analysis are just a few of its names. Call it what you, like this affliction manifests itself through one or more of the following symptoms:

o   you just can't get started,
o   you can't come up with an idea,
o   you have too many ideas,
o   you don't have an outline,
o   you can't figure out how to write an outline,
o   you have an outline but it doesn't work,
o   your characters bore you,
o   your writing is perfect,
o   you don't know what comes next,
o   your story took a wrong turn and you can't get it back,
o   you're afraid people will say your story sucks,
o   you're afraid of failure,
o   you're afraid of rejection,
o   you're afraid of success, and so on.

That list is hardly exhaustive but you get the idea. Writers say and do all the same things while wallowing in our self-induced pity party for one.

Our rallying cry?

"You just don't understand. I can't write!"

Writers are fickle critters. Our vivid and often prolific imaginations run wild given the slightest provocation.

We lose sight of reality far easier than the average person. Given our chosen profession that's a good thing but it comes at a price. We forget anything exists *outside* that vivid imagination or that it can trap us with its lies.

The biggest lie of all is we can't write. We can write. We can *always* write. We just need a reminder of that undeniable fact now and then.

Are you the instant gratification type? Do you need my guaranteed solution to writer's block this very moment? Then jump to the chapter "Slaying the Demon." Don't worry. It is safe to skip every word between this introduction and that chapter. You will still get your money's worth.

More, actually.

First, a word of warning. If you jump to there now you will miss a lot of good humour. I'm a very funny guy.

Anyway, as I said, I guarantee my simple 3-step solution will work, provided you follow my instructions to the letter. No exceptions. Note I do not say the solution is *easy*. Simple and easy are not interchangeable, not in this context.

So what's all the stuff between this introduction and that guaranteed solution, Christopher?

It's to help me, the writer, and you, the reader, comprehend the mental gymnastics we torture ourselves with for no good reason. We can see them with our eyes wide open.

We're writers. Filling endless pages with our stories, our experiences, our vision for the future... It's what we do. But we don't write because we want to write. We write because we *must* write. We're driven to it, yes, like that proverbial moth to a flame. We can't help ourselves.

Damn. Let me rephrase that by speaking solely for myself. I write and I love to write, but it's because I can't *not* write. I'm miserable when I don't write.

Just ask my wife.

George Orwell explains my dilemma perfectly.

"Writing a book is a horrible, exhausting struggle, like a long bout of some painful illness. One would never undertake such a thing if one were not driven on by some demon whom one can neither resist nor understand."

I cannot think of a more perfect Hell than one where I cannot write. I lived that hell in the form of a day job that sucked 16 hours out of me each and every day, and my creative will along with it. For a writer… for *this* writer… living thoroughly bereft of creativity was a slow, agonizing and terrifying death.

You know that terror, too, don't you? That sense your last remaining creative spark abandoned you some time back. It's sickening.

There is a solution, though.

Walk with me.

Let me show you, once and for all, how to extricate yourself from that Hell and never return.

"Who is more to be pitied, a writer bound and gagged by policemen or one living in perfect freedom who has nothing more to say?"

— Kurt Vonnegut

Defining The Problem

"Then he went into the dining room, consulting his watch. It was ten thirty already. More than half the morning was gone. More than half the time for sitting and trying to write the prose that would make people sit up and gasp. It happened that way more often now than he would even admit to himself. Sleeping late, making up errands, doing anything to forestall the terrible moment when he must sit down before his typewriter and try to wrench some harvest from the growing desert of his mind."
— *Richard Matheson, Collected Stories, Vol. 1*

Richard Matheson nailed it here.

"...and try to wrench some harvest from the growing desert of his mind."

I've been terrorized by that growing desert of my mind far more often than I care to admit. It's terrorized you too, I'm willing to bet. You wouldn't be here otherwise, so let's get right down to it.

Wikipedia defines writer's block this way:

> *Writer's block is a condition, primarily associated with writing, in which an author loses the ability to produce new work or experiences a creative slowdown. The condition ranges in difficulty from coming up with original ideas to being unable to produce a work for years.*

Writer's block is a *condition*. Sounds so mild, doesn't it? A condition is hardly even a *thing*. Oh, we writers know better. It's a thing, all right. It's a real thing. And no mild thing either. It's damned serious.

Webster's Dictionary Defines writer's block as

"the problem of not being able to think of something to write about or not being able to finish writing a story, poem, etc." and "a psychological inhibition preventing a writer from proceeding with a piece."

This is okay stuff. Not great stuff, but okay. The part about *not being able to think of something to write about* bothers me. Makes me sound like a whiny little bitch.

The phrase *a psychological inhibition* isn't much better. Still sounds like I'm making it up in my head, not actually suffering. But I *am* suffering. You are too, right?

Dictionary.com defines writer's block as

"a usually temporary condition in which a writer finds it impossible to proceed with the writing of a novel, play, or other work."

I can't speak for you but at times it doesn't feel all that temporary to me. They use that nasty word "condition" again, too. Regardless, this definition still makes me feel like a whiny little bitch.

Nope.

Don't like that definition at all.

The Urban Dictionary defines writer's block as

"A usually temporary psychological inability to begin or continue work on a piece of writing."

Now we're getting somewhere. It's a *psychological inability*! That's a *thing* for sure. I'd bet money on it. Better yet, it's not even my fault! I'm *psychologically unable*. How awesome is that?

I'm not alone in my suffering either. I'm surrounded by the most brilliant authors of all time. The list is truly staggering. In fact it scared me to even consider myself in the same room as these folks.

Leo Tolstoy, Virginia Woolf, F. Scott Fitzgerald, Charles M. Schultz, Katherine Mansfield, and Joseph Conrad, to name but a few, were all terrorized by the same demon I face. The same demon you face.

Here are a few snippets on the subject from some incredibly talented and successful writers.

"What I try to do is write. I may write for two weeks 'the cat sat on the mat, that is that, not a rat.' And it might be just the most boring and awful stuff. But I try. When I'm writing, I write. And then it's as if the muse is convinced that I'm serious and says, 'Okay. Okay. I'll come.'"
— Maya Angelou

"Writing is 90 percent procrastination: reading magazines, eating cereal out of the box, watching infomercials. It's a matter of doing everything you can to avoid writing, until it is about four in the morning and you reach the point where you have to write."

— Paul Rudnick

"Writer's block is my unconscious mind telling me that something I've just written is either unbelievable or unimportant to me, and I solve it by going back and reinventing some part of what I've already written so that when I write it again, it is believable and interesting to me. Then I can go on. Writer's block is never solved by forcing oneself to 'write through it,' because you haven't solved the problem that caused your unconscious mind to rebel against the story, so it still won't work – for you or for the reader."

— Orson Scott Card

"The best way is always to stop when you are going and when you know what will happen next. If you do that every day ... you will never be stuck. Always stop while you are going good and don't think about it or worry about it until you start to write the next day. That way your subconscious will work on it all the time. But if you think about it consciously or worry about it you will kill it and your brain will be tired before you start."

— Ernest Hemingway

"The secret of getting ahead is getting started. The secret of getting started is breaking your complex overwhelming tasks into small manageable tasks, and then starting on the first one."

— Mark Twain

"Now, what I'm thinking of is, people always saying 'Well, what do we do about a sudden blockage in your writing? What if you have a blockage and you don't know what to do about it?'

Well, it's obvious you're doing the wrong thing. In the middle of writing something you go blank and your mind says: 'No, that's it.' Ok. You're being warned, aren't you? Your subconscious is saying 'I don't like you anymore. You're writing about things I don't give a damn for.' You're being political, or you're being socially aware. You're writing things that will benefit the world. To hell with that! I don't write things to benefit the world. If it happens that they do, swell. I didn't set out to do that. I set out to have a hell of a lot of fun.

I've never worked a day in my life. I've never worked a day in my life. The joy of writing has propelled me from day to day and year to year. I want you to envy me, my joy. Get out of here tonight and say: 'Am I being joyful?' And if you've got a writer's block, you can cure it this evening by stopping whatever you're writing and doing something else. You picked the wrong subject."

— Ray Bradbury

As you see, opinions on writer's block vary even among the giants of our craft.

Now that we have a little context, let's take a look at the many variations of writer's block, shall we?

Writer's Block Takes Many Forms

Writers are creative people and as a result we've come up with dozens of variations of Writer's Block. What follows is not a complete list by any means, but it covers the major themes.

Blank Page Syndrome

"Unfortunately, many people suffer from BPS - Blank Page Syndrome. Let's face it: starting to write is scary. Seeing the cursor blinking at you on that bright white screen, realizing that you now have to come up with three or ten or twenty pages of text all on your own - it's enough to give anyone a major case of writer's block!"

— *Stefanie Weisman*

Syndromes. There are thousands of them covering every malady known to the human race. Derealization, Autophagia, Synaesthesia, Amputee Identity Disorder, Oniomania, Walking Corpse Syndrome (*yes, really*), Paris Syndrome, Jerusalem Syndrome, Capgras Delusion, Fregoli Delusion and Cotard Delusion are just some of the strange things our minds do to us if we're not careful.

Do we really need another syndrome just for writers?

No, writers don't need their own special syndrome and we don't need medication, either. We're plenty weird already. Seriously.

Look, I sit alone in a room, pound on my keyboard and make up lies until someone opens the door and drags me kicking and screaming from the room.

And that's just on my good days. On my bad days someone has to drag me kicking and screaming *into* the room. I get it. It's silly. But an honest-to-God syndrome?

No thanks.

I Can't Come Up With an Idea!

"Don't waste time waiting for inspiration. Begin, and inspiration will find you."

— H. Jackson Brown Jr.

Similar to Blank Page Syndrome, when I complain I can't come up with any decent ideas it means I'm not paying attention to the world around me. To paraphrase Orson Scott Card, we walk past a thousand ideas every day. Grab one of them already, will you?

But I don't know what to write about, you complain.

Ultimately, who cares? Just get your butt into that chair and start pounding on the keys. Surely to God something will come out. Does it matter if I start with this?

"There's a dead body on the ground. I don't know where and I don't know why."

Of course not. One of my very best scenes recently started with these very words. Impressive stuff, isn't it? No doubt about it. And I only wrote *those* atrocious sentences because I had to get something, anything onto the page.

I had no idea what to write. I knew who was in the scene but not why, not what they had to do with the dead body on the ground or even why the dead body was on the ground in the first place.

None of it.

I stared at those two sentences for a long time. A very long time.

I read my character profiles for the two people in the scene. Then I stared at my artistic renders of those two characters. (I create images of my main characters with a log line of who they are and what they want. More on that later.)

I stared at the images, read who they were and what they wanted in life. Then I stared at the screen some more until the magic happened.

I began to write.

I pounded those keys until something came out and I must tell you, what came out was amazing. It is one of the best scenes I've written in a long time. It will open my next book. Yeah. It's that good. But I had no idea where to start when I sat down at my desk.

You've been there too. I'd bet money on it.

I Have Too Many Ideas

"I don't get writers block. I get 'writer has too many ideas and doesn't know which one to start next' block."
— *Tyler Hojberg*

I have too many ideas is merely the opposite of I don't have any ideas. When I have too many ideas I allow myself (*yes, it is a choice*) to sit there, paralyzed, unable to write a word about any of them.

Sounds pretty silly when I describe it that way, doesn't it?

Pick one idea. It doesn't even matter which one. Just pick one and start writing it. If it sucks, toss it away and pick up the next idea. Sooner or later one will pan out.

My outline isn't finished or my outline isn't perfect yet.

Perfectionism is the enemy of productivity. My outline will never be perfect nor will it be complete. An outline is always a work in progress, usually until the day *after* the book is published.

But I started an outline, which means I know at least one scene my book requires, right?

Right.

When I whine my outline isn't finished or it isn't perfect it means I don't want to write. It means I want to do anything *except* write.

Pretty dumb, given my chosen career.

Here's the thing.

If I only have a single line in my outline I still have enough to begin writing. Or I can complete the outline. While that isn't writing, at least it's in the ball park. A completed outline will take me where I want to go, too. I just need to stop complaining how imperfect it is and start writing the things I must write anyway.

Now is probably a really good time to start, too. Go figure.

I Don't Know What Happens Next

When I say I don't know what happens next I actually feel stupid. Looking at those words on screen leaves me feeling ashamed of myself, and for good reason.

No writer knows what will happen next. My outline only takes me so far before I must do the dirty deed. I must sit down at my desk. Once seated I must pound those keys until everything my story requires from that scene is on the page.

When I claim I don't know what happens next I've forgotten the story I told you just a few pages back in "I Can't Come Up With an Idea!"

Not only did I not know what happened next, I didn't know what happened at all. At that point I would have happily killed for the problem of not knowing what happens next.

An idea will come.

It always does.

Why?

Because I'm a writer. Pulling ideas out of nowhere is what I do. It's my calling, my gift. It's my sacred duty, for God's sake!

Am I going to let God down by complaining?

My answer had best be a resounding *"No Sir!"* as I plant my butt in my writing chair to do my job.

People Will Say This Story Sucks

My story sucks. People will hate it. Yup, that's how this one starts. My solution, though, is perfect. I'll show them. I won't write at all.

Brilliant.

If I think my story sucks and will be universally reviled then I have one of two problems. Either my inner editor has said way too much before it's time to edit or I am correct and my story really does suck.

Either way the solution to my problem is not to cry in my beer and do nothing. My job is to fix the story problems and get on with it. If people say it sucks after I've done my best, so be it.

What the heck do they know about writing anyway?

My Characters are Dull and Boring

If I think my characters are dull and boring I have only one person to blame. It's not my inner editor, either. It's me.

Like so many other forms of writer's block this boils down to me not wanting to do my job. I'm procrastinating. I'd best sort out the reason why so I can get on with the task at hand, namely finishing my book.

Creating characters takes time for me. I'm am not one of those writers who can start the process and have an interesting and compelling character ten minutes later. I struggle but if I give up on character creation before my character says "Wow!" to me then I'm ripping off me and my readers.

I strive to embrace it, to learn more about character creation every time I start a new project. Right now, for example, I'm using a new process to create characters for my latest story. It's time consuming (*yeah, like I was so speedy in the first place*) but I'm finding it very effective.

I must concentrate on finding the joy in every step of the process. Yes, even though creating characters, building an outline and designing a world for my characters to play out their story aren't my favourite parts of writing.

Writing is my favourite part of writing.

My dilemma is this: if I don't create the characters, build a solid outline and create an interesting world for them to explore then I don't have anything to write. Guess I'd better get to it.

My Inner Editor Says I Suck

"If I waited for perfection, I would never write a word."
— Margaret Atwood

My inner editor is a bit of a bitch. It's okay. He knows I call him a bitch. That doesn't stop him from riding me. You know the drill.

"You can't write."

"You suck."

"You at this again? I thought I told you to quit and get a real job."

"If you can't even get this sentence right why don't you just die already and put me out of my misery?"

Yeah, my inner editor is one bitchy little girl whose theme is always the same.

You're not good enough.

That bitchy little girl ignores the Number One Rule of Writing. The purpose of a first draft is to puke crap onto the page. That's all. My inner editor insists every sentence must be perfect right out of the gate or there's no sense writing it at all.

Utter hogwash. Honestly. I must remind him of William Stafford's advice:

"Lower your standards and keep writing."

Solid advice. Only when I finish the first draft will I listen to my inner editor. He has no business getting involved in a first draft of anything.

I wish he would get the damn memo.

Fear of Failure

"Don't get it right, just get it written."

— James Thurber

Fear of failure, fear of success, fear I won't finish the book, fear I will finish the book, fear I won't get it published, fear I will get it published and, of course, fear nobody will read it, if and when if I do.

The corpses of writers who succumbed to their fear of failure overflow literary graveyards the world over. And what about that damn elephant taking a dump right there in the middle of the room. You know the one.

I don't have anything important to say.

Ouch. My inner editor was right. I should just kill myself already. Maybe I'll just slap him unconscious instead. Yeah, that's a much better choice.

I have something to say. Something *important*, even.

The mere fact I live and breathe means I have something positive, something profound even, to say to the world. Unfortunately sentiments like "I don't have anything important to say" have enormous power. As long as I believe that garbage it remains true.

I manufacture that awful reality just as easily as I create an alternate one when I tell myself "I have something important to say."

Every writer has something to say. It may be profound. It may be cynical. It may be funny or it may tear your heart out. It could even be all four combined.

You know I'm right, don't you?

Fear of Rejection

"I went for years not finishing anything. Because, of course, when you finish something you can be judged."

— Erica Jong

I remember my first rejection slip like it was yesterday.

Three short words on a note paper-clipped to my returned manuscript.

Unsigned.

Not for us.

I thought my story was perfect so those three little words were… *unpleasant*. I still have that note somewhere. I have a bad habit of keeping things like that.

Rejection is part of my life even when my job title is not "writer." As a writer it's just part of the deal, just as 15-hour days and sleep deprivation were part of the deal with my old job.

If I'm so paralyzed by the fear my book might be rejected before I've even written it I've stabbed my writing career right in the heart. Worse, I've done so on purpose.

Sounds pretty dumb when I put that way, doesn't it?

But what if nobody reads my book? my fear of rejection insists.

How will I ever know if I don't finish? I won't, plain and simple. Instead I'll be sitting here, wallowing in my beer, whining, instead of completing my book.

The thing is, I'm free to quit being a writer any time I want, right? Absolutely. You are too.

Not today though. Today I'm a writer and I'm not about to allow a stupid little fear get in my way.

"By the time I was fourteen (and shaving twice a week whether I needed to or not) the nail in my wall would no longer support the weight of the rejection slips impaled upon it. I replaced the nail with a spike and went on writing."

— *Stephen King*

Solid advice from the master.

Heed it. Or not.

Your choice.

Fear of Success

"If you wrote something for which someone sent you a check, if you cashed the check and it didn't bounce, and if you then paid the light bill with the money, I consider you talented."

— *Stephen King*

Success is scary, isn't it? But, as Stephen King says, if you've earned money from your writing, even a measly ten bucks, you've got talent.

I recall the first time I received a check for my writing. I was ecstatic. Over the moon, even. I can't remember the amount, but it wasn't much, maybe $25, but to me it was everything. It was *validation*.

Those few dollars proved I was a real writer.

So here's the thing. Why was validation from some unknown third party so important to me? Good question. I don't know. I was a real writer before that check arrived, truth be told. So are you.

Here's a short exercise I play with myself from time to time. Give it 60 seconds right now, then I'll share what I came up with.

Sit down, close your eyes and envision how your life will change when you sell your book to a publisher in exchange for a big fat royalty check. Or to thousands of adoring Amazon fans in exchange for their cold, hard cash? Will that success change your life?

Write down everything you will do with the money you make from your first published book.

My answers? Not much will change. I already quit my job to write full time. The money means I can pay the bills without wondering what I'll have to sell to make ends meet or if I'll go back to my old job.

So I ask you again, if you're suffering from writer's block, what's holding you back? What's the absolute worst thing that can happen after you publish your book?

Nobody will buy it? Nobody will read it? Explain to me how that is any different than right now, this very minute? Nobody's buying your book *right now*. Nobody is reading it either. The only difference is why.

They're not buying your book right now, they're not reading your book right now because you refuse to allow it.

Think about that for a minute. Do you really want to be the reason nobody buys your book? I sure hope not.

Now imagine something else. Imagine someone buys your book. I guarantee that will be the happiest moment of your writing career. That first sale will be like that check I received so long ago. That validation changes everything.

Or you can sit there, unpublished, crying in your beer and whining about how tough you have it.

It's so much easier to be the tortured artist, isn't it? Sure, but it's also a lot poorer creatively.

Nothing breeds success like success. You can't write your fourth book until you've written your first three. And you can't write your second book until you've published your first.

So get on with it already. Plant your butt in your writing chair and pound on those keys until you're done. You can thank me later, when you send me a copy of your masterpiece. I can't wait to read it.

What do these forms of Writer's Block have in common?

I'm afraid. Writer's Block is just a fancy way of saying I'm too scared to sit down and do my job. That sucks. It's also pathetic, but that's an entirely different book.

Fear is your personal enemy. Fear is the enemy of your creativity. Slay that demon any way you can. Slit its throat, stab it in the heart, shoot it in the head or poison the bastard if that's your preference, but kill the damn thing already.

I'm serious. Kill it right now.

If you're too timid, if you don't want to get your hands bloody there is an alternative that's almost as effective.

Ignore it.

Every time your fear raises its demonic little head to speak, ignore it. Eventually it will raise its head less and less often.

I'm a guy. I prefer to get my hands bloody. I chopped off its head, stuffed it and mounted it on the wall as a warning to others.

The wall mount makes me smile.

Always a bonus.

"I guess in the end, it doesn't matter what we wanted. What matters is what we chose to do with the things we had."

— Mira Grant

Popular Yet Ineffective Coping Mechanisms

Writers are pretty resourceful folks. The mental contortions we perform to avoid doing our job is astounding. What follows are some coping mechanisms used by writers to keep the beast of writer's block at bay.

Fair warning. Some of these suggestions are amusing. Downright hilarious, to be honest. Others have some merit. Others are downright moronic. All avoid the solution to the problem.

Talking With Other Writers

Every occupation has its pitfalls, its hazards if you will. What better way to learn those pitfalls than by talking with others in your chosen profession?

Writers love to commiserate with other writers over their lot in life. They're called writing conventions. You can feel sorry for yourself surrounded by people who understand your pain. Whether this pity party helps you overcome your refusal to sit down at your desk to do your job is another matter.

We are far too willing to accept our shared reality when we're when surrounded by other writers. We refuse to face the hard truth. Get on with the job at hand and write your book or carry on feeling self-important.

Is squandering your precious writing hours on meaningless blather the solution? Of course not.

Too many writers are content to squander their precious writing hours. Don't be one of them.

Class Discussion

Classroom discussions have their place but only if the person leading the discussion is willing to dish up a hard dose of reality. Students must be pushed toward success, not doomed to abject failure before they even start.

Giving students permission to believe in something as debilitating as writer's block is tantamount to educational treason. Any teacher doing so ought to be taken out behind the school, blindfolded and shot for their acts of sabotage.

Group Discussion

Group discussion is no different than talking with other writers, except the group is not comprised exclusively of writers.

This is even worse for the aspiring writer since the group will buy in to the garbage they peddle. Group members may not be intuitive enough to parse a load of horse dung from the truth. They may enable the writer's innate desire to feel sorry for him or herself.

This must not be permitted. If you are a member of such a group and a writer blathers on about how tough it is to come up with new ideas, how difficult their job is and how they suffer endlessly, do them and yourself a huge favour.

Toss a glass of cold water in their face, call them out for the cowards they are. Tell them to shut up, sit down at their desk and do their job. Writing is their chosen profession, so just get on with it already.

Leave the pity party to the professionals.

Journaling

Journaling can help get to the root of what's bothering you. It is writing, so in that sense there is value. It is not the writer's job however. Nobody will pay you for your thoughts on how rough you have it and nor should they.

Journaling is, at best, another way for writers to avoid writing.

If you must journal, here's a great way to turn it into a useful writing tool. Save journaling for the end of your day. Write down everything you felt, list everything you accomplished then write out what you hope to accomplish tomorrow.

These are good and valid uses of journaling.

List Making

Someone floated the idea of list making as a treatment for writer's block. I'm not sure why. You can make lists all day long. It's still not writing. I suppose it does have one benefit, though. At least your butt is in your writing chair.

Brainstorming

Like many other things claimed to be cures for writer's block, brainstorming is part of the outlining process. If you face story problems once the writing phase is underway then revisit your planning processes. Fix the problem at the source.

Mind-Mapping

Mind mapping, like brainstorming, is part of outline creation. Creating an outline is not writing. It's the preparation we do well in advance of writing. Anyone who claims otherwise should be ignored.

Free Association Writing

The purpose of free association writing is to take the pressure off, so in that respect it has great value. You set a timer for 15 minutes then write continuously for the duration. You stop only when the alarm goes off.

This accomplishes two things. First, it gets your butt in your writing chair. Second, it forces you to write non-stop for 15 minutes.

Free association writing delivers a bonus, as well. You might discover ideas for your current or future stories.

Now get back to the task at hand, okay? Finish the book you started.

You can't publish what you don't finish.

You can't sell what you don't publish.

Got it?

Stop Writing

When you can't write the solution is to stop writing.

I'm unclear how you stop doing what you already stopped doing. Clearly the purveyor of this snake oil is a far brighter bulb than the mere mortal standing before you. If it's a distraction you're after, dive in.

I'm a visual guy. It comes from decades in the film industry. I can waste *hours* creating an image in Smith-Micro's Poser and still come out the other end feeling creatively fulfilled. Aside from its value as a writing distraction, creating an image in Poser has the side benefit of being useful down the road.

I use Poser to build character reference images. I take a generic model, gussy it up with a specific texture, add hair, clothes, shoes and whatever weapon they use in my story. Then I pose the character in a dynamic way that expresses who they are. Add an appropriate background to the scene and I'm done.

I need to see my characters posted on the wall, like casting does in film. While I'm not a Poser Pro by any means, I can translate most of what I see in my head onto my screen. I post these on my blog, so take a look if you're interested.

Later I'll discuss how creating character reference images paid off in a scene I had no idea how to write. If you're *already* not writing a side trip into fantasy-land to bring your characters to life is a pretty cool distraction. It ain't writing but it helps when you finally get your head on straight.

Get out of Your Chair, Dance, Run or Walk

Writer's block suffers search no more. Dance, run or walk your way out of writer's block!

There are many reasons to go for a walk, a run, a half hour of Tai Chi. The human brain doesn't focus well for longer than 20 or 30 minutes at a time. Multiple studies researching how we learn prove this. These same studies reveal the type or duration of the break is pretty much irrelevant. It can be as simple and as quick as standing up, stretching your arms and sitting back down. Seriously.

Your brain says to itself, "I've had a break" and is happy to get right back to work. While this is not a cure for writer's block it is definitely a practice to consider incorporating into your everyday writing life.

That's why the Pomodoro Technique is so effective. It forces me to regularly take a break. Thing is, I need to be writing in order to take a break from writing, so...

Eliminate Distractions

Eliminating distractions is not a method for curing writer's block. Eliminating distractions is Writing 101. I don't know anyone who can write effectively with the television blaring in the living-room and the radio screeching in the kitchen, do you?

Didn't think so. Next up, writing advice for crazy people...

Write Early in the Morning

This idea is the death-knell for anyone who, like me, is normal. Don't let the fact I wrote this sentence at 9am muddy the water for you.

Some folks are morning people. While I understand these creatures exist I do not comprehend why they believe mornings are good for anything other than sleep. They're not.

If you believe mornings are glorious (like my wife) then start writing at 6am. Schedule your coffee break for 8am and lunch for 10 or 11am. Back to work at noon and another coffee break at 2pm. Pound that keyboard until 3 or 4pm and then... *Miller Time*.

For the more civilized among us a far better solution is up next.

Write Late at Night

It is GLORIOUS! You see, I'm a *civilized* human being. Normal, even. Mornings are for sleep. Nights are for writing. You know, *civilized*.

For folks like me (and perhaps like you) need to ease into my day.

I can't rush it. There is plenty of day to go around so why work myself into a lather just because its noon and I haven't written a word? That's plain crazy.

Write at a Different Time Each Day

I don't know about you but this is a no-brainer for me. Writing at a different time every day is just what I do. There are consistencies, of course, but nothing carved in stone. I write every day. That's my consistency. The times I write vary wildly.

If you are normally a slave to a writing routine alter your schedule each day for a week or two and see if the shake-up helps you. Since you're already not writing, it can't hurt to give this a shot, right?

Write While You Sleep

Cue my hysterical laughter. I am unclear how you write while you sleep and the originator of this technique didn't elaborate. I'll leave you to figure out what writing while you sleep might mean.

I'm going back to bed.

The Glass of Water Technique

Cue my hysterical laughter again. One person suggested drinking water before bed as a cure for writer's block. All I gleaned from this suggestion was a trip to the bathroom in the middle of the night.

I'm not convinced.

Here's the full idea. Pour yourself a glass of water before bed. Hold up that glass and speak some positive affirmation at it, then drink half the glass. When you wake up in the morning guzzle down the remainder and start writing immediately.

The inventor of this technique admits this one is *"a little out there."*

On that we can agree.

Waiting for Inspiration

Sit there like a bump on a log and wait for inspiration to show up?

We've found the winner of this year's *World Dumbass Award.*

I'm Too Tired

I'm too tired is not a solution to writer's block. It's a complaint twisted into a rationalization for not writing. If I'm too tired to write and it's 8am I should go back to bed. If I'm awake at 8am I ought to do that regardless. I'm a night owl. Sleeping at 8am is sensible.

However, if you're one of those weirdos who self-identifies as *morning person* this is a serious problem. You need to sort out what's wrong with your story and fix it, fast.

Talk to Your Imaginary Friend

Whoever came up with the idea of talking to your imaginary friend clearly doesn't understand the way the world works for writers. Imaginary friends come with the territory. We talk to imaginary friends all day long.

Is writer's block is when our imaginary friends stop talking to us?

Hmmm… Just might be on to something there.

Swear like a Trucker

I love this suggestion but then I already swear like a trucker. I know it's a character flaw, a sign of a lazy mind and I shouldn't do it. I'm working on it, okay?

If you don't swear like a trucker this just might be a way to let go a little and meet your inner demon. Everybody has one. If you've not seen yours in a while give this a shot. You can learn a lot if you are open to them. Who knows, they might even give you a great idea for that scene you're stuck on.

My jocularity aside, if swearing like a trucker helps you release tension then it's a great thing. We can't write effectively when we're frustrated or upset. Writing effectively requires a calm mind and a rested body.

There I go again. I forgot to add the two most important words to that sentence. Let me try again.

Writing effectively requires a calm mind and a rested body, for me.

There. That's better. It may not be true for you and it is rude of me to suggest otherwise.

Use a Different Writing Tool

Yeah, that will solve writer's block, right?

"The problem is not with me, my dear Brutus, but with Microsoft Word! If only I used Scrivener instead all my problems would be over."

The whole point of a writing tool is that it does NOT get in our way.

Switching to a writing tool I'm not familiar with only exacerbates the problem. Now I'm focused on the writing tool and how I can make it do what I need. I should be focused on writing instead.

In case you missed it allow me to clarify. I think this is one of the stupidest suggestions I've ever heard.

I hope it wasn't yours.

Take A Trip

If the point of going on the trip is to give you a change of writing venue there are far easier and less expensive ways to jolt yourself into action.

Go hang out at the local biker bar and write. You'll have an awesome environment to spark your creativity and more characters than you could possibly hope for, even on your best day of character creation.

Or you could wander down to the bus station and write.

As with the biker bar, you'll have lots of characters to choose from. The upside is a potentially less hostile environment. Bonus points!

While these suggestions have merit, I urge you to wander over to your nearest coffee shop instead. Find yourself a quiet corner and set up shop. The staff will be supportive and deliver you more caffeine than you ought to drink but the clientele will ignore you completely, which brings me to…

The Caffeine Slam

I was not a coffee drinker until a few years ago. Now I love the stuff. When I read about the coffee slam as a cure for writer's block I just had to give it a shot. After I stopped laughing, of course.

The idea is simple. Set a timer for 20 minutes. Slam a cup of coffee. Start the timer and write. When the timer goes off, stretch your legs, grab another cup of coffee, slam it, reset the timer and do it again.

Do this 3 or 4 times in a row and you'll never complete 20 minutes of writing. You'll be too busy running to the bathroom.

Write Somewhere Else

Changing your writing venue can jump-start your creativity, as I touched on in previous entries. One blogger even suggested abandoning your writing desk in favour of some new location was *a proven cure* for writer's block.

I fail to see how. I deliver The Proven Cure for Writer's Block in this very book!

Mental stagnation is a problem every writer faces. Switching up writing locations is as good an idea as any for solving that problem, but I doubt it's a cure for writer's block.

Why? There's an old saying that's always stuck with me. It rears its ugly head whenever I want to move to get away from my troubles, real or imagined.

Wherever you go you take yourself with you.

What a crappy thing to say, right? Sure takes the wind out of my sails.

Something to think about, though, the next time you want to change writing locations because you fell for the lie "*I'll write so much better somewhere else.*"

Write in Your Local Bookstore

Writing in your local bookstore or coffee shop is great if you want a change of venue but as I explained in the previous entry, wherever go you take yourself with you.

While the change of scenery can be a great motivator, if all it takes is a different view to cure your writer's block I would suggest you're not blocked at all, just bored.

Time to come up with a fresh idea and write about that.

Wash the Dog

My wife thinks this is a sure-fire cure for writer's block. I'll let her tell you in her own words.

"I guess if it's a choice between washing the dog and writing, I'd write too."

Damn, she's good.

Wash the Car

Here my wife goes again.

"Have you ever even washed your car?"

Nice. I'd say something rude here but she's liable to read over my shoulder and slap me.

Need to get a lock on my office door, I swear.

Shut Off Your Computer

This idea is right up there with "Use a Different Writing Tool" to cure writer's block.

I write with a computer because my typing keeps up with my brain. This keeps my internal editor out of the loop. If I turn off my computer and use a pad of paper instead I will not complete a sentence. My infernal editor will rewrite it seven times first.

Not really the solution when my goal is to complete a first draft.

If you need a break, take a break. Grab a coffee or a juice or a glass of water (talk to it if you must) and get back to work.

Now that's some solid advice, unlike the notion of shutting off the one tool you actually use for work.

Idiots!

Browse Old Photo Albums

This is a suggestion that is more procrastination than a cure for our dreaded malady.

Unless you're writing about mom, Dad and Uncle Sammy looking through old family photos won't help you do anything but reminisce. Not that there's anything wrong with reminiscing. There isn't. But it ain't no cure and it sure ain't writing.

Play on Facebook

Ah, here's the solution! Spend time on the biggest time-sucking social media vortex of all: CrackBook.

I use Facebook for two things: to promote my writing and to find current events to blog about.

Damn... I just proved this idea's creator was right. I went for ridicule and wound up with "*Ah Ha!*" instead. I hate that.

Okay, how about this. Writing current events commentary is not the same as writing a novel. How's that for rationalization? Pretty good, right?

My own issues aside, if you're wasting your time on Facebook and think it will miraculously cure your writer's block you are fooling yourself.

Do this right now. Shut off your internet connection. You can't turn it back on until you've written a thousand words. Same goes for your cell phone.

How's that for incentive? You'll have two thousand words in no time.

Re-Read Your Best Work

This idea makes a ton of sense. I'm positive in days past you wrote some amazing things. Yes, even you, the pathetic sad sack huddled in the corner sobbing. Even you must admit that much, right?

So grab your best writing, be it a blog post, book chapter or poem and re-read it. Remind yourself you are not a talentless hack who should kill yourself immediately but an incredible writer with amazing skill and talent.

Re-reading our best work is worthwhile even if we are *not* huddled in the corner sobbing and can't figure out what to write next.

Start in the Middle of the Story

One of the beautiful things of working from a detailed outline is you can write anywhere in your story. You're not committed to starting at the beginning because you already know that. You know the end as well, so plopping yourself down in the middle of your story and writing your heart out is absolutely fine.

This doesn't technically qualify as a coping mechanism either, since you are writing. Even if it's not what you thought you'd write when you sat down to begin your work day.

Hmmm… but you *are* sitting at your desk writing, aren't you?

Excellent.

Take a Smoke Break

Haven't you heard? *Smoking Kills.* Do something else, *anything else,* instead.

Listen to the Rain Pelt Down on a Tin Roof

My wife laughs at me whenever a thunder storm passes through. I run out the front door and stand under our tin-roofed gazebo. I practically dance, I'm so happy to hear thunder crack all around me. The sound of the rain as it pounds down on the metal roof above my head is glorious. Truly.

It's no cure for writer's block but, if you're like me, it will definitely bring you immense joy. What better way to get those creative juices flowing than immense joy?

Remember my insanity the next time a thunder storm rolls through your town. Even if you don't have a tin roof to stand beneath, run outside and dance in the rain.

Your neighbors will think you are nuts. Who cares? You're a writer. You knew you were nuts already. And all that dancing while getting completely drenched? It's wonderful for the soul.

Steal Someone Else's Idea

Stealing someone else's idea is the cornerstone of all writing, isn't it? One school of thought says there are only seven original stories. If that's true every writer since the Stone Age copied one of them and wrote their own version.

Ernest Hemingway wrote, *"In any art you're allowed to steal anything if you can make it better."*

Hollywood says *"Nothing shall be done for the first time."*

Look at how movies are pitched. Originality? Why bother?

"Think Indiana Jones meets Thelma and Louise."

Writing someone else's idea is better than not writing at all.

Read a Book

Reading a book merely delays the inevitable. The flip side is you cannot write if you do not read. Unless you read every day, preferably in your chosen genre or field, writing effectively for your audience is all but impossible.

It hearkens back to that notion of stealing someone else's idea. Reading other writers in your genre sparks all kinds of creative thoughts. It also exposes those ideas you should never, ever write because they are so overdone and clichéd.

Here's the deal. Reading is not a suggestion for writers, it's imperative.

But it's not writing.

Listen to Music

Listening to music is a good idea for writers. Listening to music, specifically classical music, forces the brain into its most creative and problem-solving mode. I discuss this later in the chapter titled *"Actions guaranteed To Help."*

It also helps you focus on the task at hand.

Isn't greater focus and more creativity what every writer wants?

Read Inspirational Quotes

Reading inspirational quotes is procrastination, pure and simple.

Nothing wastes more time and is less productive than reading the words of another writer on the subject of how to be inspired to write.

What an *atrocious* sentence. It's on par with this suggestion.

Unless you bought my book *"TOP SECRET: Inspiration, Motivation and Encouragement – 701Essential Quotes for Writers"* of course.

Then it's an excellent suggestion.

Defining The Solution To Writer's Block

I take issue with the coping mechanisms described in the previous chapter because they do not deal with the root problem. They deal with the symptom of that problem.

By focusing on symptoms instead of resolving the underlying problem, those coping mechanisms allow me, the writer, to sit in a corner mewling like a kitten. It allows me to feel sorry for myself instead of forcing me to do what I was born to do: write.

So how about we slay that demon once and for all?

In the next chapter I provide my 100% Guaranteed Solution to writer's block but I feel it is only fair to warn you.

This solution is not for the faint of heart.

It's for writers.

"Why do I keep evading my work?
Is it because I'm afraid of being
confronted by my lack of abilities?"

— Candace Bushnell

Slaying The Demon of Writer's Block

"We are what we repeatedly do. Excellence, therefore, is not an act but a habit."

— Aristotle

There are countless mental aberrations today, primarily due to a societal need to label *everything*. Medication is prescribed for a myriad of mental deficiencies. We're sick and drugs will make us better, right?

Lies. Great big steaming piles of lies.

We aren't sick. We don't have a mental aberration either. Our chosen profession does not count. Our only problem is our stubborn refusal to sit down and do our job.

Okay, you whine. *I'll try to write something.*

Try? You need a good swift kick in the butt from my favourite Jedi Knight, Master Yoda.

"Try not. Do. Or do not. There is no try."

It shocked me to learn I quoted him incorrectly for years. I paraphrased his timeless truth thus:

"There is no try. There is only do."

Either way, the point is made.

Do.

There is no try.

"The art of writing is the art of applying the seat of the pants to the seat of the chair."

— Mary Heaton Vorse

Writer's block is a self-induced mental dilemma designed to keep you immobile and stagnant. The solution is for you, the writer, to take correct action, just as Mary Heaton Vorse explained.

"What is hell to a writer? Hell is being too busy to find the time to write or being unable to find the inspiration. Hell is suddenly finding the words but being away from your notebook or typewriter. Hell is when the verses slip through your fingers and they never return again."

— R.M. Engelhardt

Step 1 - Plant Your Buttocks in Your Writing Chair

"Do not wait to strike till the iron is hot; but make it hot by striking."
— *William B. Sprague*

Step 1. Plant Your Buttocks in Your Writing Chair

If your butt ain't in the chair you ain't gonna write. It's that simple.

Your brain needs motivation so give it some.

Plant your butt in a chair.

Place your chair in front of your computer.

Turn on your computer.

Step 1 is easy, right?

Of course it is.

So is Step 2.

"A deadline is, simply put, optimism in its most kick-ass form. It's a potent force that, when wielded with respect, will level any obstacle in its path."

— Chris Baty

Step 2 - Set a Deadline

"Inspiration is a guest that does not willingly visit the lazy."
— *Pyotr Tchaikovsky*

Step 2. Set a Deadline.

I don't care what the deadline is. Five minutes, ten minutes or even just one single minute, if you're feeling particularly horrid. Think you can handle that? Think you can handle pounding your keyboard for a whopping 60 seconds?

Great.

Set your timer.

If you don't have one, follow this link.

http://ChristopherDiArmani.net/Free-Writing-Timer

It's free. I wrote it.

You can have it.

Download it, then fire it up.

Now it's time for the master stroke. That's Step 3.

You're going to love this part.

"Confront the page that taunts you with its whiteness. Face your enemy and fill it with words. You are bigger and stronger than a piece of paper."

— Fennel Hudson

Step 3 - Write

"The best way in the world for breaking up a writer's block is to write a lot."

— John Gardner

Step 3. Start the timer. Write until the timer expires.

It doesn't matter what you write.

Write garbage. Write masterpieces. Write anything. Give yourself permission to write absolute sewer trash if you must, so long as you write *something*.

You made a deal. If it would rid you of writer's block you said you would follow my instructions to the letter.

You committed to writing until the timer goes off. So do it already.

Start the timer and write.

Don't even read the rest of this chapter.

Just WRITE!

Okay, so you won't listen to reason. I get it. I really do.

Here's the simple, unadulterated fact of a writer's life.

You overcome writer's block by writing.

Shocking, I know. Writing is work, just like any other job, so we must quit our bitching and get down to it.

Barbara Kingsolver puts it rather eloquently.

"I learned to produce whether I wanted to or not. It would be easy to say oh, I have writer's block, oh, I have to wait for my muse. I don't. Chain that muse to your desk and get the job done."

Darynda Jones is a little more to the point, even if she softens her advice with a touch of humour.

"Real writers write. Period. No, the muse does not come to visit everyday. She's a lazy, precocious flirt. You cannot get into the habit of being 'in the mood' to write. No writer on Earth is in the mood to write everyday, but the good ones do it anyway. They fight through their fatigue, their stress, their doubt, and they write. They get the words on the page. Period. So stop waiting for your muse. Trust me, she sleeps around."

As awesome Darynda's advice is, and it is awesome, I find Philip Pullman's brutal directness more my style.

His contempt is lit by the flamethrower he uses to belch Hellfire down upon the feeble. While his imperious decree may offend some, those poor offended souls cannot hide from the truth Philip Pullman mercilessly delivers.

"Writer's block...a lot of howling nonsense would be avoided if, in every sentence containing the word WRITER, that word was taken out and the word PLUMBER substituted; and the result examined for the sense it makes.

Do plumbers get plumber's block? What would you think of a plumber who used that as an excuse not to do any work that day? The fact is that writing is hard work, and sometimes you don't want to do it, and you can't think of what to write next, and you're fed up with the whole damn business.

Do you think plumbers don't feel like that about their work from time to time? Of course there will be days when the stuff is not flowing freely. What you do then is MAKE IT UP. I like the reply of the composer Shostakovich to a student who complained that he couldn't find a theme for his second movement. 'Never mind the theme! Just write the movement!' he said.

Writer's block is a condition that affects amateurs and people who aren't serious about writing. So is the opposite, namely inspiration, which amateurs are also very fond of. Putting it another way: a professional writer is someone who writes just as well when they're not inspired as when they are."

The solution to writer's block in a single sentence. It's beautiful.

"A professional writer is someone who writes just as well when they're not inspired as when they are."

You call yourself a writer?

Great. Plant your butt in your chair, turn on your computer and *write*.

I, for one, cannot wait to read it when you're finished.

That's It.

I told you the solution was simple. Not *easy*, but simple.

Writing is work.

Deal with it.

Our most valuable trait is also our greatest weakness. Our imagination screams in terror the instant we cast our eyes on a blank page. We race off to a fantasy Sahara Desert where ideas are more precious than a single drop of water.

We die of thirst, happily, like fools.

We manufacture story problems where none exist. We ignore obvious and simple solutions in favour of some elusive Holy Grail of Story Fixes. In short, we allow our imagination to run wild instead of behaving like a professional — He plants his butt in his chair and does what he was born to do: he writes.

> *"I think writer's block is simply the dread that you are going to write something horrible. But as a writer, I believe that if you sit down at the keys long enough, sooner or later something will come out."*
> — *Roy Blount, Jr.*

While the solution to Writer's Block really is as simple as planting your butt in your chair and writing, there are things you can do to stave off your more delightful excuses and procrastinations.

In the next chapter I suggest ways you can make writing as stress-free as possible, along with some techniques to jump-start your writing day.

Actions Guaranteed to Help

"Somebody said that writers are like otters… Otters, if they do a trick and you give them a fish, the next time they'll do a better trick or a different trick because they'd already done that one. And writers tend to be otters. Most of us get pretty bored doing the same trick. We've done it, so let's do something different."

— *Neil Gaiman*

There are concrete steps you can take to improve your writing and your writing habits. Some are easy. Some are hard. All will help you write better and more consistently when you apply them to your craft.

If you're not writing as well as you desire, if you're not writing as consistently as you should, what do you have to lose by following these suggestions?

Just your writing career.

Nothing very important, right?

Face The Truth About Writing

"A writer is someone for whom writing is more difficult than it is for other people."

— *Thomas Mann*

That is the cold hard truth. Writing is work. Writing well is even harder work.

Walter Mosley says, *"If you want to be a writer, you have to write every day."*

If you do not write every day you cannot become a better writer. You do want to become a better writer, don't you?

To be blunt, claiming writer's block as an excuse for not doing your job is both stupid and rude. It's stupid because you *chose* to be a writer.

Nobody held a gun to your head and said *write or die.*

No. You chose it. Or, what's far more likely, writing chose you. It's in your blood. You must write and you feel terrible when you don't. Believe me, I get it. Been there. Done that.

"A winner is someone who recognizes his God-given talents, works his tail off to develop them into skills, and uses these skills to accomplish his goals."

— Larry Bird

Ignoring your God-given talent is rude. When you are given a gift your duty is, first, to say thank you, and second, to work your tail off to hone your talent into skill and use your skill to accomplish your goals.

Simple. Besides, nobody wants to be stupid and rude at the same time.

Writing is work. Sometimes easy work, sometimes hard work, sometimes joyous and delightful work and sometimes painful and horrendous work. Sounds like every other job when I put it that way, doesn't it?

Accepting writer's block as inevitable and incurable is plain dumb. Here's why. When I lay claim to it the only person stopping me from writing is me. If that's not the stupidest thing ever I'm not sure what is.

I'm a writer.

Do I hear coal miners whine about how tough their job is? Do they complain they have coal miner's block and can't do it today? No. They get on with it and do what must be done.

I'm a writer.

If it's 9am on Monday morning I must do what everyone else does at 9am on Monday morning.

Show up for work, on time, and do my job.

Write Every Day

"I only write when I am inspired. Fortunately I am inspired at 9 o'clock every morning."

— *William Faulkner*

Challenge yourself to write every day. Create a blog and dare yourself to write one new article every day. You will be amazed how quickly this turns your writing career around.

Years ago I struggled to write consistently. I created a blog and committed myself to write one article each and every day.

Was it difficult? At first, absolutely. I had all the usual doubts.

What will I write about?

I can't do this.

It's too hard.

My inner editor spewed useless advice relentlessly. Thank God I never listened. I just wrote my article and published it every single day.

That commitment delivered an answer I didn't even know I sought. Writing one blog post every day made all my other writing easier. The reason is obvious. I'd already solved the dilemma of what to write about. I was in writing mode already so whatever other writing I had on my plate that day was easier.

"Just write everyday of your life. Read intensely. Then see what happens."
— *Ray Bradbury*

There was another unexpected benefit too. While I wrote the blog for purely for myself, within weeks it became a source of inspiration for others concerned with the same issues that concerned me. I earned a following.

The third benefit was unsolicited writing jobs. I wasn't even looking for writing jobs when I started the blog. I just wanted to write consistently and improve my craft, two of the most selfish of reasons imaginable.

"Discipline allows magic. To be a writer is to be the very best of assassins. You do not sit down and write every day to force the Muse to show up. You get into the habit of writing every day so that when she shows up, you have the maximum chance of catching her, bashing her on the head, and squeezing every last drop out of that bitch."
— *Lili St. Crow*

I don't agree with those who preach write *5 days a week and take 2 days off* to give your creativity a break. Those 2 days off are the death knell for me because those 2 days will stretch into 3, then 4 and so on…until I'm not writing at all, despite my intentions to the contrary.

"Exercise the writing muscle every day, even if it is only a letter, notes, a title list, a character sketch, a journal entry. Writers are like dancers, like athletes. Without that exercise, the muscles seize up."

— *Jane Yolen*

Write every day. If you only write 500 words per day at the end of the year you have 182,500 words under your belt.

Sounds so easy when I put it that way, doesn't it?

Now, what words should you write every day? That's next.

Write From an Outline

"Sit down to write what you have thought, and not to think about what you shall write."

— *William Cobbett*

The single most effective tool in my writer's toolbox is my outline. Creating an outline is also, for me, the hardest part of writing. It's where I must figure everything out.

I love an outline because deep down I'm lazy. I want things to be simple. I want things to be easy. More than anything I just want to sit down and write and write and write until my fingers bleed and my eyes no longer focus.

I'm at my absolute best as a writer when I'm in that zone. The outline is how I get into the zone and stay there.

By doing the hard work up front I take away any possible excuse. How can I sit on the couch and whine "I don't know what to write" when I have an outline? I can't. I know what to write. It's all right there in front of me. All that's left is to fill in the blanks and enjoy the process.

That appeals to both my innate laziness and my desire to pound the keys until my fingers bleed and my eyes no longer focus.

If you do enough planning before you start to write, there's no way you can have writer's block. I do a complete chapter by chapter outline.
— *R.L. Stine*

Honestly, writing from a well-planned outline is the simplest and fastest way to write any book. Fiction, non-fiction... it doesn't matter.

For fiction writers the outline is where you create your characters, sort out what will happen to them along their journey, figure out why they do what they do and solve all your story's problems.

For non-fiction writers the outline is where you work out what you want to say and the order you want to say it. It covers every idea for your chosen subject, presented in an orderly fashion.

It is impossible to get stumped because it's all there in front of you, perfectly planned out, in advance.

"The secret of getting ahead is getting started. The secret of getting started is breaking your complex overwhelming tasks into small manageable tasks, and then starting on the first one."
— *Mark Twain*

I completed the first draft of this book in under a week because I wrote a detailed outline first. I knew what I wanted to say. I knew the order I wanted to say it. Then I wrote all night long until my fingers bled and my eyes no longer focused. I am a night owl, remember?

Authors who write from a clear outline will tell you this is the easiest and fastest way to write. It's also the single best way to take Writer's Block and smash it to pieces with your trusty old Underwood typewriter. Deeply satisfying, too.

Schedule a Specific Time to Write

"The one ironclad rule is that I have to try. I have to walk into my writing room and pick up my pen every weekday morning."
— *Anne Tyler*

I include this step with trepidation. Here's why.

I don't do it. I *can't* do it. Not consistently.

There are reasons for that. Actual valid reasons, not the usual made-up drivel I tell myself to keep me from writing.

When I'm working on a movie, for example, set life demands 15-hour days and a constantly changing schedule. Finding a consistent time to write is difficult when you start work on Monday at 7am and by Friday you don't begin until 5pm.

Even now that I've quit the day job to write full time I don't do it.

My writing schedule most days goes like this. I wake up at the crack of 9am or so and fire up the Keurig machine. French Vanilla is my current favourite, followed closely by Hazelnut. My wife is a fan of Costa Rica, both the country and the coffee.

While the Keurig does its thing I meander into my office and fire up my computer. The computer comes to life slowly, like me, so I wander back into the kitchen and grab that mug of freshly-brewed coffee. A touch of cream, a dash of sugar and I'm good to go.

I read my Bible, check my email, scan the news, read whatever Slashdot has on its radar... You know, simple stuff that allows my brain time to adjust to daylight. After an hour or so I'm ready to work. Well, most days. Some days it takes a little longer, others a little less but you get the idea.

I write for a few hours and take a break. That could be to shower (always a good idea!), to chop firewood or do pretty much anything that needs doing while giving me a short break from writing at the same time.

My wife comes home from work and we talk a while before she goes off to unwind, then I write until dinner. We eat and spend time together until she goes off to bed, usually by 9pm. Around 10pm I wake up. I mean *seriously* wake up. If I'm awake at 10pm I won't sleep for another 4 hours minimum. So I hit the keyboard hard and before I know it the clock says something rude like 2am. Often 4 or 5. Seldom midnight or 1.

I keep pounding that keyboard until my fingers bleed and my eyes refuse to focus. Or is it my eyes bleed and fingers refuse to focus? Either way, when I can no longer function I crawl into bed and lapse into my daily coma.

You can't call it sleep.

Around 9am the next day I open the coffin lid, crawl out and the process starts all over again. There is no hard and fast schedule though. I will happily sleep 'til noon if I can.

When I'm on a deadline I barely sleep. Maybe 5 hours a night if I'm lucky. I'm also one of those oddball writers where my subject matter can dictate what time of day I can write. Not always, mind you, but sometimes.

If I'm writing a current events commentary or a non-fiction book then my daily writing schedule described above works flawlessly. I wake up in the morning, make myself a cup of coffee, read my Bible and email, etcetera, and get to work. No problem.

I'm a strange duck. I accept that. Let me give you an example.

Certain subject matter is impossible for me to write if the sun shines. When I wrote my first vampire movie I completed the outline during the day. When it came time to actually write the script, that's when everything fell apart.

For the first 3 or 4 days I beat the crap out of myself because I could not plant my butt in my chair and write. Even if I could get my butt planted in my chair I would do anything *except* write.

It was horrible.

By the 4th or 5th day I figured it out. You see, during those first days I did write. I just couldn't do it until the sun was over the horizon. Once the sun set I pounded those keys until the birds started chirping at 3:30 in the morning. They're amazingly loud and annoying when you're struggling to finish a scene before you collapse from exhaustion.

When I realized that particular story could only be written at night, everything changed. The revelation, and it truly was a revelation, released me from the self-abuse I heaped upon myself those first few days.

I could to do whatever I pleased while the sun was up, knowing the moment it dipped below the horizon I would be at the keyboard for the next 6 hours. And that's exactly what happened. I completed the entire 120-page script in 21 days. Nights, actually.

A mind is truly a strange place.

While I personally fail at a consistent writing routine, writing at the same time every day, I see the value of that consistency. Writing is my job and like any job I must show up for work on time, right? Nod your head and say it with me.

"Yes, Christopher, I must show up for work, on time, every day."

There, that wasn't so hard, was it? What *time* of day I write daily isn't nearly as important as the consistency of writing every day, regardless of start time. This pearl of wisdom from Norman Mailer adds one more layer to that consistency.

"Over the years, I've found one rule. It is the only one I give on those occasions when I talk about writing. A simple rule. If you tell yourself you are going to be at your desk tomorrow, you are by that declaration asking your unconscious to prepare the material. You are, in effect, contracting to pick up such valuables at a given time. Count on me, you are saying to a few forces below: I will be there to write."

As Mailer suggests, I commit to writing the following day. I make notes about what to write and what to research, then I go to bed. A deep comfort washes over me, brought on by the knowledge I prepared myself for what tomorrow will bring. It continually amazes me how this simple nightly task increases my daily productivity while diminishing my innate desire to procrastinate.

Create Mini-Deadlines For Yourself

"A hammer made of deadlines is the surest tool for crushing writer's block."

— *Ryan Lilly*

Long before I learned of the Pomodoro Technique I knew mini-deadlines were useful. I was a computer programmer in a past life so I one day I built myself a writing timer. I use it when I'm struggling to get my writing day underway.

My writing sessions can be timed anywhere from 1 to 30 minutes.

I currently favor a 15 minute session. That's short enough I don't feel stuck there forever and long enough for my writing to get on a good roll.

I consistently write just over 300 words of fiction in a 10 minute session. It's almost bang on 312 words every time. When I use a 15 minute session I consistently write around 600 words.

I don't understand it. I merely accept it and set the timer for 15 minutes. Might as well get double the output for two-thirds the time commitment.

Sometimes the timer will go off and scare the crap out of me. I am so focused on writing that I forget about it. I feel pretty silly when I jump out of my chair, absolutely. Then I laugh out loud and carry on writing.

"I love deadlines. I like the whooshing sound they make as they fly by."
— Douglas Adams

My brain is hardwired to meet deadlines. It doesn't matter that the deadline is artificial. Once I click the start button I must write. In fact, once I start that timer I cannot *not* write.

If your brain works the way mine does then I encourage to you visit my website and grab a copy of my free writing timer. I give the timer away for free so if you want a copy download it from here:

http://ChristopherDiArmani.net/Free-Writing-Timer

Minimize Distractions

Minimizing distractions is really simple. Notice once again I did not say easy. We love our procrastinations. I'm as guilty of that as any writer, maybe more. Given how easily I can be distracted by some passing shiny object, I must enforce an environment to minimize those shiny objects.

1. Shut my office door. I have a sign on the door that says *"Novelist At Work. Do Not Disturb."* Sometimes my wife even respects the sign and the closed door upon which it rests. Sometimes.

2. Turn off my Internet connection. The Internet is my personal Black Hole of Time. Facebook, Twitter and email are time-sucking vortexes with no redeeming value.

3. Turn off my phone. That way I cannot be distracted. If the caller has something really important to say they will leave a message.

Don't worry, my writing friend, I hear your screams. They're my screams too, especially when it comes to shutting off the Internet. Trust me, research can and should be done before I sit down to write and there is nothing happening on your phone that can't wait for a few hours.

4. Put on music. Classical. Something with no words. Or at least not words you can understand. Lately my preference is Gregorian Chant.

5. Set a timer. If I can't get my butt in gear I start my trusty writing timer and set a deadline. The actual deadline doesn't matter. Ten minutes, an hour. Same difference, really. The purpose of starting the timer is to put me under the pressure of a deadline. That forces me to begin. Mission accomplished.

Essentially I lie to myself. I commit to writing for ten minutes. That's all. I tell myself I only have to write for ten minutes, knowing full well that once I get my fingers in gear I will be there for hours. That's what I call a good lie. It gets me writing.

Listen to Non-Verbal Music

"I just sit at my typewriter and curse a bit."
— P.G. Wodehouse

To stave off the cursing I listen to classical music, and not just because I like it. I find my concentration and focus is better when I listen to classical music. I am also less susceptible to mental fatigue.

Studies prove listening to classical music aids in concentration and creativity. Researchers at Stanford University conducted a study found *"music engages the areas of the brain involved with paying attention, making predictions and updating the event in memory. Peak brain activity occurred during a short period of silence between musical movements - when seemingly nothing was happening.*

"In a concert setting, for example, different individuals listen to a piece of music with wandering attention, but at the transition point between movements, their attention is arrested," said the paper's senior author Vinod Menon, PhD, associate professor of psychiatry and behavioral sciences and of neurosciences."

The *New York Times* also examined the effect of music on the brain.

In biological terms, melodious sounds help encourage the release of dopamine in the reward area of the brain, as would eating a delicacy, looking at something appealing or smelling a pleasant aroma, said Dr. Amit Sood, a physician of integrative medicine with the Mayo Clinic.

People's minds tend to wander, "and we know that a wandering mind is unhappy," Dr. Sood said. "Most of that time, we are focusing on the imperfections of life." Music can bring us back to the present moment.

"It breaks you out of just thinking one way," said Teresa Lesiuk, an assistant professor in the music therapy program at the University of Miami.

Dr. Lesiuk's research focuses on how music affects workplace performance. In one study involving information technology specialists, she found that those who listened to music completed their tasks more quickly and came up with better ideas than those who didn't, because the music improved their mood.

"When you're stressed, you might make a decision more hastily; you have a very narrow focus of attention," she said. "When you're in a positive mood, you're able to take in more options."

If your default is to write in silence I encourage you to put on some classical music and see what happens. Your productivity might just get that bump you want, along with increased peace of mind.

Sources:
https://med.stanford.edu/news/all-news/2007/07/music-moves-brain-to-pay-attention-stanford-study-finds.html
http://www.nytimes.com/2012/08/12/jobs/how-music-can-improve-worker-productivity-workstation.html?_r=0

Create Your Personal Writing Sanctuary

"Serious writers write, inspired or not. Over time they discover that routine is a better friend than inspiration."

— Ralph Keyes

One of the greatest gifts you can give your writer self is a writing sanctuary or writing den. This is a comfortable environment where you feel safe and secure to write without interruption.

My computer has three monitors; one for writing, one for research and one for music and anything else I need on display.

The view out the window is my mountain and on really good days I'll find myself interrupted by a lynx, coyote, bear or deer as they wander through the yard.

Yes, there are worse places to write.

While I have not done so yet, I'm toying with the notion of using the local coffee shop as my writing sanctuary. Other writers find it helpful to focus in a different environment than their normal writing space. You may want to try that too.

Wherever you choose to write, it must be a safe place you can write uninterrupted for long periods of time.

Final Thoughts

"Just write every day of your life. Read intensely. Then see what happens. Most of my friends who are put on that diet have very pleasant careers."

— Ray Bradbury

We writers are blessed. It's a calling, a gift from God, if you like. Why we insist on making it so hard for ourselves is beyond me, yet we do.

The single greatest gift you can give yourself as a writer is the certain knowledge that writer's block does not exist. It's a fallacy; a silly notion invented by a brilliant writer to explain to his irate boss why he missed his deadline.

Unfortunately his irate editor bought into the lie and a whole subculture of writing maladies were born.

Lies. All lies.

Writing is a job. Like any job you must show up every day, on time and work. It's that simple and that hard.

I will leave you with these wise words from William Faulkner. Ignore them at your peril.

"Don't be a writer; be writing."

"The public is wonderfully tolerant.
It forgives everything except genius."

— Oscar Wilde

One Last Thing!

First, thank you for reading this book!

If you enjoyed this book (and even if you did not) I would be grateful if you would post an honest review on Amazon and/or Goodreads. Every review helps this book find more readers, the lifeblood of any author. The links are below.

http://christopherdiarmani.net/Review-Writers-Block-Goodreads

http://christopherdiarmani.net/Review-Writers-Block-Amazon

Your support in the form of an honest review on these sites really does make a difference. I also read every review as part of my efforts to can make my books even better.

I would also be grateful if you shared this book on Google+, Facebook, Twitter, Pinterest and Goodreads.

If, for some reason, you did not like this book or didn't get what you expected out of it please tell me directly so I can use your constructive criticism to update the book to meet your expectations. You can contact me here:

http://ChristopherDiArmani.net/Contact/

Thank you so much for your support, feedback and your honest reviews.

Sincerely,

Christopher di Armani
Author Extraordinaire
http://ChristopherDiArmani.net/Books

About Christopher di Armani
"Author Extraordinaire"

The hardest writing for any author, I suspect, is writing about themselves. It sure is for me. I can write the most personal quirks and embarrassing situations for any character in my fiction. Writing about myself is… uncomfortable.

I'm not one for the spotlight. I like the shadows. I'm most comfortable there. Most writers are.

Writing is my passion and I'm my happiest when I'm pounding out a story. Like many writers I am an avid reader. My earliest memories are of Zane Grey westerns. I devoured them like candy. His strong male characters, no matter their personal flaws, always did the right thing when it counted. That is what drew me to his books. I imagine I learned a lot of my own moral code from the characters Zane Grey created.

Like many writers I am an introvert. Do not allow the protestations of past co-workers convince you otherwise. They see what I want them to see – the social face that allows me to function out in the world.

Every writer has one. It's how we survive until we make our way back to the safety and security of our writing room.

I am a good writer. That's not arrogance speaking. That's a fact substantiated by the money folks pay me to write. Bad writers don't get paid.

I didn't start off a good writer though. My first novel, written when I was 16, is proof of that. It's about teenage gangs in high school, about bad choices and worse friends. I wrote it as an assignment for English class. My teacher took pity on me and commended me for its length and ambition with a C Plus.

Notice he did not say *talent*.

The book is horrible. Really. I stumbled across it a few years ago and attempted to read it. By the end of the first page I wanted to vomit. It's trash. I accept that.

I started writing young and wrote anything that struck my fancy. Some published, most wasn't. I wrote letters to the editor, newspaper articles, short stories, poetry, novellas, books, short films and feature-length screenplays.

Major newspapers, both print and digital, published me as time passed and talent increased.

Then I edited a national magazine for a firearms advocacy group for two years. That's where I learned first-hand just how hard we writers make it on our editors. During my tenure as magazine editor I learned how to edit *anything* into readable form fast. Why? I had to meet deadline.

That's a lesson that serves me well to this day.

I'm also a huge horror movie fan. I love vampires (*not the ones that sparkle*), werewolves and scary guys like Hannibal Lector. My interests vary as do my forms and genres of writing. I love writing current events commentary. That love turned into a book on the RCMP's ongoing issues as well as a book on Canada's 23rd Prime Minister, Justin Trudeau.

I've written a vampire movie and a series of two serial killer movies and I'm turning all three scripts into novels. I just finished the first draft of the novel based on the vampire script. When I finish that I'll turn the two serial killer movies into novels and add the third and final installment to that series.

Along the way I'm sure I will write other odd things, too. Like most writers I too have more ideas than I have time to write.

That's the joy of the creative mind, isn't it?

I also love art but cannot draw to save my life. Hold a gun to my head and say "draw or die" and I'll make my peace with God while awaiting your bullet. The good Lord gave me many talents but drawing is not one of them.

That's why I love Poser, a 3D image creation and animation program. It allows me to fulfill my artistic desires despite my complete lack of artistic ability.

As a writer I love Poser. I use it to create character reference images for my characters. I have a concrete vision of who my characters are, what they look like, what they wear, how they hold themselves, etc. Poser gives me the power to translate the vision in my head onto my computer screen. I print them out, pin them to the wall and ponder them when I need inspiration.

If you've managed to reach the end of this wandering diatribe I both thank you for your patience and commend you for your perseverance. There's nothing worse than reading about someone droning on about themselves!

Since you're still here I'd love to keep you updated about what I'm writing next. Just visit my website below.

http://ChristopherDiArmani.net

Until our paths cross again…

Christopher di Armani
Author Extraordinaire
http://ChristopherDiArmani.net/Books

Books by Christopher di Armani

The Simple 3-Step Secret to Slaughter Writer's Block And Vanquish it Forever

We writers are fickle beings. Or at least we can be. Our minds are impressive places. Our vivid and often prolific imaginations run wild given the slightest prodding and we lose sight of reality far more easily than the average person.

That's not a bad thing. It's actually a huge benefit given our chosen career. But that fickle imagination can also trap us with lies.

The biggest lie of all is that we can't write. We can write. We can always write. Sometimes we just need to be reminded of that simple fact and my Simple 3-Step Secret is just the ticket when Writer's Block has you under its thumb.

Top Secret - Inspiration, Motivation and Encouragement 701 Essential Quotes for Writers

This book is a compilation of 701 quotes covering 39 aspects of writing and the writing life. Within its pages you will discover quotes to make you laugh and bring a tear to your eye. Some will be as familiar as an old friend, others will be brand new. The common theme is this: we writers are the same no matter what we write about and we learn from one another.

It's meant as a resource for writers in need of inspiration or encouragement late at night or early in the morning. It's meant to cheer you up as well as make you think. Above all it's meant to build a deep desire to write inside you.

Justin Trudeau - 47 Character-Revealing Quotes from Canada's 23rd Prime Minister and What They Mean for You

On October 19, 2015 Canadians elected their 23rd Prime Minister based on good looks, nice hair and a famous name. They voted for style over substance.

Our 23rd Prime Minister's entire leadership experience consisted of teaching snowboarding lessons and high school drama. His management experience consisted of administering his trust fund and his ego.

Not a single thought was given to what he stood for, what his party stood for, or what he would actually do once elected to the highest office in the land.

That bothered me. That bothered me so much I began to research his much-publicized missteps and that in turn revealed a disturbing pattern within Trudeau's numerous faux pas.

That pattern is the focus of this book.